A Little Brazilian Cookbook

Elisabeth Lambert Ortiz

ILLUSTRATED BY JOSÉ GERALDO FAJARDO

First published in 1992 by
The Appletree Press Ltd,
7 James Street South, Belfast BT2 8DL.
Copyright © 1992 The Appletree Press, Ltd.
Illustrations © 1992 The Appletree Press, Ltd.
Printed in the E. C. All rights reserved.
No part of this publication may be reproduced
or transmitted in any form or by means,
electronic or mechanical, photocopying,
recording or any information and retrieval
system, without permission in writing from
the publisher.

A Little Brazilian Cookbook

First published in the United States in 1992 by
Chronicle Books, 275 Fifth Street,
San Francisco, CA 94103

ISBN 0-8118-0110-1

9 8 7 6 5 4 3 2 1

Introduction

Brazilian cooking is exuberant and varied, reflecting the history and geography of this vast country. In the north, in Bahia de Todos Os Santos, there is an exciting mixture of the food of the Guaraní Indians, the colonizing Portuguese and African slaves. Portuguese cooking is influenced by Europe and the Middle East, Africa contributed okra and *dendê* (palm oil), and the Guaraní brought cassava meal (*manioc*), peanuts, and cooking methods to the kitchen. Further south in Rio de Janeiro the national dish, *Feijoada Completa*, was created. West of Rio, the cuisine of the state of Minas Gerais is more European but the use of indigenous foods transforms it into something inherently Brazilian. The coastal waters are rich in fish and shellfish. In the far south there are magnificent beef cattle, and the *churrascarias* (city restaurants) serve meats from wall-size grills. In the country there are barbecues where whole animals are cooked on the spit. Brazilians have a sweet tooth which reflects the Moorish influence in Portuguese food which is translated into Brazilian rich cakes and desserts. And was there ever such coffee? Strong, sweet and aromatic, it is served in small cups, ready to be drunk at any hour.

A note on measures

Spoon measurements are level except where otherwise indicated. Seasonings can of course be adjusted according to taste. Recipes are for four, unless otherwise noted.

3

Massa para Empadhinas

Pastry for Little Pies

Little savory pies and turnovers are a great favorite in Brazil and are eaten at all hours, along with cakes and small cups of strong coffee. Made small, they make an ideal first course. Larger versions make fine main courses for lunch.

5oz plain flour
½ tsp salt
1 oz lard, cut into bits
1 oz unsalted butter, cut into bits
1 large egg yolk
2 tbsp cold water, about
1 small whole egg
(makes about 15)

Sift the flour and salt into a large bowl and rub in the lard and butter with your fingertips to make a coarse meal. Make a well in the center and stir in the egg yolk with enough water to make a soft but not sticky dough. Cover and refrigerate for an hour. Roll out the dough on a lightly floured surface until very thin and cut into circles 1½ inches, larger than the tartlet pans to be used, and an equal number of circles the same size as the tartlet pans. Press the larger circles into the pans and fill until ¾ way up with the filling (see page 7). Beat the egg with a little water and moisten the edges of the pastry with this egg wash. Cover with the smaller circle and seal, firmly pinching with fingers. Brush the tops with egg wash and bake in a preheated moderate oven at 350°F for 30 minutes or until golden brown.

Recheio de Camarão

Shrimp Filling

There are many different fillings for *empadhinas*. This one, from Bahia, is a great favorite as prawns and shrimps are both abundant in Brazilian waters. To make the thick coconut milk, dilute packaged coconut cream to make a mixture the thickness of heavy cream. Use milk to dilute. If *dendê* (palm oil) is not available, use vegetable oil.

---

2 tbsp palm or vegetable oil
$^1/_2$ medium onion, finely chopped
$^1/_2$ medium sweet green pepper, seeded and finely chopped
I small hot red or green chilli, seeded and finely chopped
$^1/_2$lb cooked, peeled frozen shrimp, defrosted and chopped
2 fl oz coconut milk
I large egg yolk
I tbsp fresh coriander, finely chopped
salt
(makes 15)

Heat the oil in a frying pan and sauté the onion, pepper and chilli until soft. Take off the heat and add the shrimp. Beat the egg yolk with the coconut milk and stir it into the shrimp mixture. Stir in the coriander, season to taste and cook over low heat until the mixture has the consistency of medium thick white sauce. If necessary, thicken with $^1/_2$ teaspoon of cornstarch mixed with a little water. Cool and use as a filling for little pies.

Acaraje

Black-eyed Pea Fritters

Black-eyed peas, which are really beans, originated in Africa and were brought to the New World by African slaves. Fritters made with the beans are popular in the Caribbean and South America. This version from Bahia in northern Brazil is my favorite. If packaged black-eyed pea flour (*harina para bollitos*) is available, use it according to package instructions.

2 1/3 cups black-eyed peas	**Sauce**
1/2 cup dried shrimp	1/2 cup dried shrimp
1 medium onion, finely chopped	1 medium onion, chopped
salt	1 tbsp dried hot red
dendê (palm oil)	chilli peppers, crumbled
	1/2 ginger root, peeled
	and chopped
	3 tbsp dendê (palm oil)

(makes 24)

Cover the black-eyed peas in cold water and soak overnight. Drain, rub off and discard the skins. Soak the dried shrimp in cold water to cover for 30 minutes. Combine the peas, shrimp and onion in a food processor and process to a purée. Season to taste with salt, if necessary. Heat enough oil in a frying pan or deep fryer to reach a depth of 2 inches and fry the pea mixture in tablespoons until the fritters are golden brown on both sides. Drain on paper towels.
Sauce: Soak shrimp in cold water for 30 minutes. Drain, reduce to a purée in a blender with onion, chilli peppers and

ginger root. Heat oil in a frying pan and sauté mixture for 3 or 4 minutes. Serve in a bowl, to accompany the *acaraje.*

Bolinhos de Bacalhau

Codfish Fritters

Though Portugal and Brazil have magnificent fresh fish, Portugal's love of salt codfish (*bacalhau*) has been inherited by Brazil and both countries like salt codfish fritters. This is the Brazilian version.

8oz salt codfish (bacalhau)	¹/₂ cup milk
2 tbsp butter	I cup cooked mashed potatoes
I medium onion, finely chopped	2 tbsp plain flour
I tbsp parsley, finely chopped	I large egg, lightly beaten
salt, freshly-ground pepper	oil for frying

(makes about 24)

Soak the fish overnight in cold water to cover, changing the water several times. Drain and remove any skin and bones. Flake the fish with your fingers. Heat the butter in a frying pan and sauté the fish with the onion, parsley, salt (if necessary), and pepper. Add the milk, potatoes, flour, and egg and mix thoroughly. Remove from the heat and cool. Form the mixture into tablespoon-size cakes and fry in hot oil until lightly browned on both sides. Serve hot or at room temperature. Serve, if desired, with tomato sauce.

Sopa de Milho com Camarão

Corn and Prawn Soup

Brazil has splendid and abundant prawns ranging from tiny shrimps to large prawns. Corn is a staple crop. The two are used together in this recipe to make a richly-flavored soup.

---

2 tbsp butter
1 medium onion, finely chopped
1 cup cream-style sweet corn
1 1/4 cups good chicken stock
salt, freshly-ground pepper
2 cups cooked, frozen prawns, defrosted and coarsely chopped

Heat the butter in a small frying pan and sauté the onion until it is soft. Combine the onion in a saucepan with the corn, chicken stock, and salt and pepper to taste. Heat through gently, then stir in the prawns and cook just long enough to heat them through, about 1 minute. Do not overcook as they toughen very quickly.

Sopa de Feijão Preto

Black Bean Soup

The common bean, *phaseolus vulgaris*, was first cultivated in Mexico about 7,000 years ago and spread throughout the Americas long before the arrival of Columbus. Brazil grows many types of beans with black beans being the favorite. They are an essential part of the daily diet. If black beans are not available use pinto or red kidney beans.

---

1 cup beans, picked over, rinsed and soaked overnight
2 tbsp olive oil
1 medium onion, finely chopped
1/2 cup tomato, peeled, seeded and chopped
salt, freshly-ground pepper
1 tbsp fresh coriander or parsley, chopped
2 cups chicken stock

Drain the beans and put into a saucepan with enough water to cover by 2 inches and simmer, covered, until the beans are tender. Drain and measure the liquid. There should be 2 cups. Make up the liquid with water if necessary and set beans and liquid aside.

Heat the oil in a frying pan and sauté the onion until it is soft. Add the tomato and cook until the mixture is well blended. Season with salt and pepper. Add the coriander or parsley. Transfer the mixture to a food processor with the beans and some of the reserved liquid. Reduce to a purée and return to the saucepan with the rest of the liquid and the chicken stock. Heat through and serve. If the soup is too thick, thin with stock or water.

Canja

Chicken, Ham, and Rice Soup

This apparently simple soup is made special by the addition of rice, tomatoes, carrots, and chopped ham. These combine to lift the flavor out of the ordinary, making the soup a substantial one, ideal for a light meal when accompanied by a green salad and a dessert.

---

3 lb chicken, half
1 medium onion, chopped
6 cups chicken stock
1/4 cup long grain rice
3/4 cup tomatoes, peeled, seeded and chopped
1/2 cup young carrots, scraped and diced
salt, freshly-ground pepper
3/4 cup cooked ham, diced
1 tbsp chopped parsley, preferably flat continental type

In a saucepan combine the chicken, onion, and chicken stock, bring to a simmer, cover and cook over low heat until the chicken is tender (about 45 minutes). Lift the chicken out onto a platter and set aside. Strain the stock through a sieve set over a bowl. Discard the solids and skim off as much fat as possible from the stock. Rinse out the saucepan and return the stock to it. Add the rice, tomatoes and carrots. Taste for seasoning, add salt if necessary and freshly-ground pepper.

Bring to a simmer and cook until the rice is tender, about 25 minutes. When the chicken is cool enough to handle remove the skin and bones and cut into strips about ½ x 1½ inches. Return the chicken to the saucepan with the ham and cook just long enough to heat through. Add the parsley and serve.

Salada de Palmito

Hearts of Palm Salad

"Hearts of palm" are the tender heart buds of any one of several species of palm trees. They are not usually available outside the countries of origin, but an excellent canned product can be bought in specialty shops or delicatessens. It is worth searching for as the flavor is attractive and delicate.

---

hearts of palm, 1 lb can
1 tbsp lime, or lemon juice
1 tbsp Dijon mustard
salt, freshly-ground pepper
3 tbsp olive oil

Drain the hearts of palm and cut into ½ inch slices. Transfer to a salad bowl. In a small bowl beat together the lime juice, mustard, and salt and freshly-ground pepper. Whisk in the oil until the mixture is thick and well blended. Pour over the hearts of palm slices and toss lightly to mix.

Salada de Quiabo

Okra Salad

Okra, the fruit of the *hibiscus esculentus*, also known as lady fingers, was brought to Brazil by Africans who worked on the sugar plantations of the north. The vegetable quickly became popular in Mexico, the Caribbean, and into South America. This salad is unusual and refreshing.

I lb fresh young okra pods	**Vinaigrette**
salt	¹/₄ cup wine vinegar
I tbsp lemon juice	salt, freshly-ground pepper
I tbsp white onion,	³/₄ cup olive or salad oil
finely chopped	
3 tbsp vinaigrette	
salad greens	

Wash and dry the okra pods and cut away the stalk but do not cut away deeply enough to expose the seeds with their sticky juices. Drop the okra into briskly-boiling salted water with the lemon juice and cook, at a simmer, for about 8 minutes, or until the okra are tender. Drain and cool. Make the vinaigrette by combining vinegar with salt and pepper to taste. Whisk in the oil in a steady stream until the mixture is well blended. Toss with the onion and vinaigrette and serve in a salad bowl on a bed of salad greens, chopped.

Chuchu Ensopado

Boiled Cho-Cho

This member of the squash family rejoices in many names. Originally from Mexico, its name in Nahuatl was *chayotl*. This was changed by the Spanish into the widely-known *chayote*. It is also called *christophene*, *cho-cho*, *chuchu* and vegetable pear, an apt name as the vegetable does resemble a slightly prickly green pear. You can usually find it in specialty stores. The seed is edible and the cook is entitled to this tasty nibble while transferring the dish to the table.

---

2 medium-size vegetable pears (cho-chos),
peeled and quartered
salt, freshly-ground pepper
2 tbsp butter
1 tbsp fresh coriander leaves, or parsley, finely chopped

Drop the vegetable into briskly boiling salted water, return the water to a boil and simmer, uncovered, for about 10 minutes or until the vegetable is tender. Drain thoroughly and return to the saucepan with the butter and parsley. Season to taste with salt and pepper and serve hot.

Vagens

Green Beans

The Brazilian cook has a large range of vegetables to choose from. There are all the familiar vegetables of Europe, as well as the vegetables of the New World and those, such as okra, that were introduced by Africans. They are seldom served plainly cooked so dishes like this one can be served as light lunch or supper dishes, especially good for vegetarians. This is a delicious and satisfying green bean dish.

I lb green beans, trimmed and halved
salt, freshly-ground pepper
I tbsp unsalted butter
I tbsp plain flour
I cup milk
I large egg yolk, lightly beaten

Drop the beans into a large saucepan of boiling water, bring back to a boil over high heat and cook, uncovered, for about 8 minutes until the beans are crisply tender. Drain, set aside and keep warm. Melt the butter in a saucepan over low heat and stir in the flour. Cook, while stirring, and without letting the mixture brown, for 1–2 minutes. Add the milk gradually off the heat, stirring constantly to make a smooth sauce. Season to taste with salt and pepper and cook, while stirring, for 3–4 minutes, then mix in the beaten egg yolk. Pour the sauce over the beans and heat through gently for 2 minutes. Serve immediately.

Repôlho com Vinho

Cabbage with Wine

This is an unusual way of cooking cabbage which makes this green vegetable into a very appetizing and special dish. It demonstrates the Brazilian talent for adding flavor to otherwise ordinary dishes.

---

1 small head cabbage, washed and finely shredded
salt
2 tbsp olive oil
1 medium onion, finely chopped
1 small hot green or red chilli pepper, seeded and chopped
1 medium green pepper, seeded and chopped
3 tbsp chopped parsley
1 cup fresh tomato sauce
$3/4$ cup dry white wine
salt, freshly-ground pepper

Blanch the cabbage in a large saucepan of boiling salted water. Drain and set aside. Heat the oil in a frying pan and sauté the onion, chilli pepper, green pepper, and parsley until the onion is soft. Add the tomato sauce and wine, season to taste with salt and pepper, bring to a simmer and pour over the cabbage. Cover and simmer for 5 minutes over low heat or until the cabbage is tender. If necessary, add a little water to prevent the cabbage burning. Serve with any plainly cooked meat or poultry.

Peixe Assado com Vinho

Baked Fish with Wine

Fish and shellfish are favorite foods in Brazil. Portuguese are great seafood lovers and fish is a principle food for Indians of the Amazon region. Brazil has an abundance of salt, fresh-water, and shell-fish.

I whole 2 1/2 lb sea or striped bass, cleaned and scaled
2 medium onions, grated or finely chopped
1/2 cup parsley, finely chopped
1/2 tsp ground coriander seed
2 cloves garlic, crushed
2 small fresh red or green chilli peppers,
seeded and finely chopped
6 tbsp lemon juice
1/2 cup olive oil
salt
1/2 cup dry red or white wine

Combine the onions, parsley, coriander, garlic, chilli peppers, lemon juice, olive oil, and salt to taste in a bowl. Put the fish in a dish large enough to hold it comfortably and pour the mixture over it. Marinate in a cool place or in the refrigerator for 4 hours, turning from time to time. When ready to cook, lift the fish out of the marinade, pat dry with paper towels and arrange in a baking dish. Mix the marinade with the wine and pour over the fish. Bake in a preheated oven at 375°F for 25 minutes or until the fish feels firm when pressed with a finger, basting frequently with the marinade. Serve with the marinade accompanied by plain rice or *Farofa* (see page 40).

28

Moqueca de Peixe

Fish Stew

Moquecas were originally Indian dishes called *pokekas*. The food was wrapped in banana leaves and cooked over charcoal. They evolved in the great houses of the Portuguese sugar plantations and are now cooked in a saucepan on top of the stove. They are usually made with prawns, fish, or crab.

---

2 lb fillets of sole, flounder, plaice or any
white fish cut into 2 inch pieces
1 medium onion, chopped
1 or 2 fresh hot chilli peppers, seeded and chopped
2 medium tomatoes, peeled and chopped
1 clove garlic, chopped
1 tbsp fresh coriander leaves
salt
3 tbsp lime or lemon juice
$1/4$ cup dendê (palm oil) or olive oil

Put the fish into a large bowl. In a blender or food processor combine the onion, chilli pepper, tomatoes, garlic, coriander, salt to taste, and lime or lemon juice. Reduce to a purée and add to the fish, mixing lightly. Stand for 1 hour. Transfer to a saucepan and add 6 tbsp of water and half the oil. Cover and simmer for about 5 minutes until the fish is done. Pour in the remaining oil and heat for 1 more minute. Serve with rice.

Arroz Brasileiro com Mariscos

Rice, Brazilian-style with Shell-fish

Brazilians eat a great deal of rice and cook it in a special way that leaves the grains separate and firm to the bite. Rice forms the basis of many dishes, such as this one made with clams or mussels. If there is any juice from the clams or mussels, measure it and use it instead of the equivalent amount of water when cooking the rice.

---

4 tbsp olive or vegetable oil
1 medium onion, thinly sliced
1 1/2 cups long grain rice
1 1/2 cups chicken stock
1 1/2 cups water
1 medium tomato, peeled, seeded and chopped
salt
24 shucked clams or mussels, juice reserved
1 tbsp lemon juice
2 tbsp fresh coriander or parsley, finely chopped

Heat the oil in a heavy saucepan and sauté the onion until soft. Stir in the rice and cook for 2–3 minutes until grains are coated with oil. Do not let it brown. Add the stock, water (or water and fish juice), tomatoes, and salt. Bring to a boil, cover and cook over very low heat until the rice is tender and the liquid absorbed. Season the shellfish with lemon juice. Five minutes before the rice is cooked, fold in the shellfish and herbs. Cover and finish cooking.

Moqueca de Camarão

Prawns in Coconut Milk

This is a favorite Bahian dish. It shows the influences of the local Guaraní Indians and of the Africans who were brought in to work on the sugar plantations. Coconut milk can be bought canned or made from fresh coconuts. The simplest method is to dilute pure creamed coconut to the consistency of single cream.

I clove garlic
¹/₂ tsp salt
I lb large raw peeled prawns, or large frozen cooked prawns, defrosted
2 tbsp dendê (palm oil), or olive oil
I small onion, finely chopped
2 medium tomatoes, peeled and chopped
I tbsp fresh coriander leaves, chopped
I small fresh hot red chilli pepper, seeded and chopped
I tbsp lime or lemon juice
³/₄ cup coconut milk

Crush the garlic with the salt and add to the shrimp. Set aside. Heat the oil in a frying pan and add the onion, tomatoes, coriander, chilli pepper, and lime or lemon juice and simmer for 5 minutes. Add the coconut milk and cook for 5 minutes longer. If using raw prawns, add and cook for about 3 minutes, or until they turn pink. If using cooked prawns add them for I minute, or just long enough to heat them them through. Serve with Brazilian-style rice (see page 40).

Feijoada Completa

Black Beans with Mixed Meats

No book on Brazilian cuisine would be complete without a recipe for *Feijoada Completa*, the national meal, which originated in Rio de Janeiro. It comprises seven dishes as the beans and meats are served with traditional accompaniments. It deserves to be called a feast and, though a lot of work is involved, it makes a magnificent party dish. It is versatile: unavailable meats can be substituted with others. Much of the cooking can be done ahead of time.

1 pig's foot, split	**Sauce**
3 lb smoked ox (beef) tongue	2 tbsp vegetable oil
1/2 lb piece lean smoked bacon, rind removed	2 medium onions, finely chopped
1 lb piece salt (corned) beef	2 cloves garlic, chopped
4 cups black (haricot) beans, soaked overnight	2 medium tomatoes, peeled, seeded and chopped
1 lb piece lean beef chuck or bottom round	1 small fresh hot red or green chilli pepper, seeded and chopped
1 lb fresh pork sausages	salt, freshly-ground pepper
1/2 lb smoked spicy pork sausage such as chorizo	

(serves 8–10)

Cover the pig's foot in cold water to cover and simmer, covered, for 1 1/2 hours. Cool, bone, transfer to a covered container together with the cooking liquid and refrigerate overnight. Cover the tongue, bacon, and salt beef with cold water, soak overnight. Next day, drain beans and put them

36

into a saucepan or casserole large enough to hold all the ingredients. Add the pig's foot and its cooking liquid. Cover the beans with cold water by 2 inches. Bring to a simmer, cover and simmer for 1 1/2 hours over low heat. While the beans are cooking, put the tongue, bacon, and salt beef into a large saucepan with water to cover and simmer, covered, over low heat for 1 hour.

When the beans have cooked for 1 1/2 hours add the bacon, salt beef, and fresh beef, but leave the tongue to simmer separately. If necessary, add hot water to keep the beans covered. Simmer for 2 hours more. Remove the tongue from the heat and when cool enough to handle, peel and remove any gristle and bones. Add the tongue to the bean pot with more hot water if necessary. Stir the beans from time to time to keep them from sticking. Prick the fresh sausages and add them to the bean pot with the smoked sausage. Simmer for 15 minutes, remove from heat.

Sauce: Heat the oil in a frying pan and sauté onions and garlic until onions are soft. Add tomatoes and chilli and cook until the mixture is thick. Season with salt and pepper. Scoop out a cupful of the beans and mash into the tomato mixture. Stir this back into the pot and simmer over low heat for 10 minutes longer.

To serve, lift out the meats and arrange them on an oval platter. Slice the tongue and put it in the center, with the slices overlapping. Slice the beef, bacon, salt (corned) beef and smoked sausage and arrange round the tongue in separate piles. Add the sausages to the platter. Pour the beans, which should be very soft, almost a soup, into a tureen. *Feijoada* is accompanied by rice, kale, *farofa*, sliced oranges, and hot pepper and lime sauce (see pages 40 and 43).

Farofa de Azeite de Dendê (Cassava with Palm Oil)

Cassava is native to Brazil and was first cultivated there by the Guaraní Indians. Popular throughout Latin America, in Brazil it is made into *farinha de madioca* (cassava meal or *manioc*). In Asian shops it is sold as *gari*. In Brazil, it is toasted to a pale brown, put into a *farinheira* (special shaker) and sprinkled on meat, poultry, and vegetables. The *farofas* are more elaborate and can be served with any main course.

---

1 cup cassava meal
2 tbsp dendê (palm oil) or butter

Toast the cassava meal in a frying pan over low heat, stirring constantly until pale brown. Do not let it burn. Stir in the oil or butter until the *farofa* is well blended and a bright orange-yellow. Put in a dish and serve with any meat or poultry.

Arroz Brasileiro (Brazilian-style Rice)

---

2 cups long grain rice	*1 clove garlic, chopped*
¼ cup vegetable oil	*3 cups water*
1 small onion, finely chopped	*salt*

Wash the rice in a saucepan in several changes of water. Drain and pour enough hot water into the saucepan to cover. Let stand for 15 minutes, drain for 10 minutes. Heat oil in the saucepan, then add rice, onion and garlic and sauté over very low heat, stirring constantly until rice is a light gold and oil absorbed. Add water and salt to taste, bring to a boil then reduce heat as low as possible. Cook, covered, until the rice is tender and the liquid absorbed.

Môlho de Pimenta e Limão (Hot Pepper and Lime Sauce)

The chilli peppers used in Brazil are the tiny, fiery hot *malagueta* peppers. The Jamaican chilli Scotch Bonnet is an admirable substitute, or any very hot green or red chilli pepper.

---

*6 small very hot red or green
chilli peppers, seeded and chopped
1 small white onion, finely chopped
1 clove garlic, chopped
4 tbsp lime or lemon juice
salt*

Crush the chillies, onion, and garlic with salt to taste in a mortar, adding the lime or lemon juice little by little, or purée the ingredients in a food processor or blender.

Couve à Mineira (Shredded Kale or Collard Greens)

Collard greens are a variant of kale, two members of the enormous crucifer family. Best described as non-heading cabbages, they can be used interchangeably.

---

*3 lb 5oz kale or collard greens, washed
2oz bacon fat, melted
salt*

Trim the leaves from the greens and shred them finely. Bring a large saucepanful of water to a brisk boil and drop in the shredded greens. Boil, uncovered, for 3 minutes. Drain in a colander, pressing down to extract all the liquid. In a large, heavy frying pan heat the bacon fat and add the greens. Season with salt and cook, stirring with a wooden spoon until the greens are tender, about 5 minutes.

Costeletas de Porco

Pork Chops

Brazilian cooks use marinades, not just to tenderize meats, but to give them extra flavor and as the basis for a lively accompanying sauce.

1/4 cup lemon juice
I bay leaf, crumbled
I medium onion, finely chopped
I clove garlic, crushed
2 medium tomatoes, peeled and chopped
2 tbsp olive oil
salt, freshly-ground pepper
1/2 small fresh hot red or green chilli pepper, seeded and chopped
4 thick-cut pork loin chops
2 tbsp butter

Purée the first 8 ingredients in a blender or food processor. Arrange the chops in a dish and pour over the marinade. Marinate for 4 hours, turning once or twice. Lift out the chops and scrape off any marinade. Pat dry with paper towels. Heat the butter in a pan, add the chops, cook on a moderate heat 4–5 minutes on each side. Remove to a serving platter and keep warm. Add the marinade to the casserole, add a little water or white or red wine, bring to a simmer and cook for 5 minutes. Pour over chops and serve with *Farofa* (see page 40).

Coração Recheado

Stuffed Calf's Heart

The south of Brazil is noted for the excellence of its beef. This dish is an enjoyable change from the usual steaks and roast beef. Calf's heart is more convenient for a small family than beef heart and cooks in a much shorter time.

---

1 lb calf's heart	1/2 small red or green chilli
2 tbsp butter	pepper, seeded and
1/2 small onion, finely chopped	finely chopped
1/4 cup corn kernels	1 tbsp parsley, finely chopped
1/4 cup breadcrumbs	salt, freshly-ground pepper
1 small hardboiled egg, chopped	1 cup dry red wine
1/4 small sweet red pepper,	1 cup beef stock
seeded and finely chopped	1 clove garlic, chopped
2 pimiento-stuffed olives,	2 tsp cornstarch or arrowroot
halved	

Wash the heart and remove fat and membranes that divide the two chambers. Pat dry. Heat half the butter and sauté the onion until it is soft. Purée the corn in a food processor and scrape into a bowl. Add the onion, breadcrumbs, egg, sweet pepper, olives, chilli, parsley, and salt and pepper to taste. Mix well and stuff into the cavity of the heart. Sew up, or skewer and lace with string. Heat the remaining butter in a casserole dish and sauté the heart. Pour in the wine, stock and garlic and bring to a simmer. Cover the casserole with foil, then a lid, and cook in a preheated oven at 350°F for 1 1/2 hours, or until tender. Lift out onto a serving platter and remove sewing

47

thread or skewers and string. Cut heart into crossways slices and keep warm. Reduce the cooking liquid to half its volume. Mix the cornstarch or arrowroot with a little water and stir into the sauce. Cook, stirring, until the sauce is thickened. Pour some over the sliced heart and serve the rest in a sauceboat. Serve with mashed potatoes and green beans or peas.

Galinha Em Yogurt

Chicken in Yogurt

Portuguese and Middle Eastern influences combine in this dish. Guinea hen is sometimes used in Brazil instead of chicken. The marinade can be used with any poultry.

1 large clove garlic, crushed	1 cup dry white wine
1/4 tsp black pepper, freshly-ground	1/4 cup white wine vinegar
1/2 tsp salt	2 1/2 lb chicken, quartered
1 medium onion, finely chopped	4 tbsp bacon fat or vegetable oil
1 clove	3/4 lb tomatoes, peeled, seeded and chopped
1/4 cup each parsley and fresh coriander leaves, chopped	1 medium onion, finely chopped
1 medium carrot trimmed, scraped and grated	1 cup plain yogurt
1 rib celery with leaves, chopped	

Combine the first 11 ingredients and mix well. Arrange the chicken quarters in a shallow dish and pour the marinade over

48

them. Marinate overnight, turning once or twice. Remove the chicken from the marinade. Reserve the marinade. Pat the chicken dry with paper towels. Heat the bacon fat or oil in a large frying pan and sauté the chicken pieces, turning once. Add onion and tomatoes and sauté until onion is tender. Add reserved marinade, cover and cook over low heat, turning the chicken pieces once, until tender. Lift the chicken pieces out onto a warm platter and keep warm. Whisk the yogurt into the sauce in the pan to warm it through. Taste for seasoning and add salt and pepper if necessary. Pour the sauce over the chicken and serve with rice. Garnish with pitted green and black olives and cooked artichoke hearts.

Xinxim de Galinha

Chicken with Shrimp and Peanut Sauce

The mixture of flavors in this Bahian dish is unusual but not so exotic that it is off-putting. Guaraní Indians provide the dried shrimps, the peanuts and the hot chilli peppers; Africans contribute the palm oil; the Portuguese provide the chicken.

2 1/2 lb chicken, quartered	1/2 cup dried shrimp, finely ground
3 tbsp lemon juice	
2 cloves garlic, crushed	1/2 cup peanuts, ground
salt	1 small fresh red chilli pepper, seeded and chopped
2 tbsp olive or vegetable oil	
1 medium onion grated	1/2 cup chicken stock
	3 tbsp dendê (palm oil)

Combine the chicken quarters with the lemon juice, garlic, and salt to taste. Set aside. In a heavy saucepan heat the oil and sauté the onion, dried shrimp, peanuts, and chilli pepper over low heat for 5 minutes, stirring frequently. Add the chicken pieces and any liquid in the bowl. Add the chicken stock, bring to a simmer, cover and cook over low heat until the chicken is tender, 30–45 minutes. Turn chicken once during cooking and add a little more stock if necessary. Pour in the palm oil and cook for 1–2 minutes longer. Serve with white rice and *Farofa* (see page 40).

Pato Em Môlho de Frutas

Duckling in Fruit Sauce

This dish has strong links with the days when the Iberian Peninsula was occupied by Arab invaders. The use of fruit with poultry or meat is characteristic of Middle Eastern cooking, and the Portuguese brought it with them to the New World, a culinary wedding.

Marinade (see **Galinha Em Yogurt** page 48)

4 lb duckling, quartered	1 1/4 cups warm water
2 tbsp vegetable oil	4oz chopped cooked ham
3/4 lb mixed dried fruit	dry red wine
(pitted prunes, apricots,	salt, freshly-ground pepper
peaches and pears)	2 tsp cornstarch

Pour the marinade over the duckling pieces in a baking dish or bowl and refrigerate overnight, turning once or twice. Remove the duckling from the marinade, scraping off the

solids. Reserve. Heat the oil and sauté the duckling pieces in a large frying pan, turning to brown slowly over moderate heat to release as much fat as possible. Lift out the duckling and discard the fat. While the duckling is browning, soak the dried fruit in warm water. Drain. Leave prunes and apricots whole, in halves or quarters. Combine the duckling pieces and the fruit, with the reserved marinade and ham, in a casserole dish large enough to hold the pieces comfortably. Pour in water in which the fruit has soaked and enough dry red wine to barely cover. Cover and simmer over low heat until the duckling is tender, about 1 1/2 hours. Add salt and pepper if necessary. Lift the duckling out onto a serving dish and keep warm. Reduce sauce over brisk heat for a few minutes or thicken slightly with cornstarch mixed with a little cold water. Pour the sauce over the duckling and serve with white rice.

Crème de Abacate

Avocado Cream

Avocados are usually savory dishes and, apart from avocado ice cream, this is the only avocado dessert I have come across. It demonstrates the originality of the Brazilian kitchen. It is simplicity itself and can be made at the last minute.

---

2 large ripe avocados
3 tbsp fresh lime or lemon juice
4 tbsp superfine sugar

Halve the avocados, remove the pits and mash the flesh in the shells with a fork. Turn out into a bowl and mash with lime or lemon juice and sugar to make a smooth mixture. Pile into glass serving dishes, garnish with a slice of lime or lemon.

Quindins de Yayá

Coconut Cupcake Dessert

Yayá was the name given by slaves on the big sugar plantations of Bahia to the young girls in the household. The cakes make a good dessert to serve after *Feijoada* (see page 40).

2 cups fresh coconut finely grated	8 large egg yolks
	1 large egg white
2 tbsp butter, softened	1 cup sifted plain flour
1 1/2 cups light brown sugar	butter

(makes 24)

In a large bowl beat together the coconut, butter, and brown sugar, mixing thoroughly. Beat in the egg yolks one by one. Beat the egg white until stiff peaks form, and fold into the mixture. Gradually beat in the flour. Butter a 24-cup cupcake pan, pour in the cake mixture and stand in a baking tin filled with water to come above halfway up the pan. Bake in a preheated oven at 350°F for about 45 minutes or until a cake tester comes out clean.

Mousse de Castanhas de Caju
e Chocolate

Cashew Nut and Chocolate Mousse

This is a wonderful mousse made especially rich with the addition of cashew nuts which, like chocolate, are native to the Americas.

2oz plain dark chocolate
$1/2$ cup sugar
5 large egg yolks
I cup cashew nuts, ground fine
I cup heavy cream
5 large egg whites
(serves 6)

Break the chocolate into small pieces and put into the top of a double boiler set over boiling water. Pour in 3 tbsp water and the sugar and stir until the chocolate has melted and the sugar dissolved. Remove from the heat and beat in the egg yolks one by one. Stir in the nuts. Beat the cream until it stands in peaks and fold into the chocolate mixture. Beat the whites until they stand in firm peaks and fold into the mixture, gently but thoroughly. Pour into a serving dish and refrigerate overnight or until set. Serve, if liked, with whipped cream.

Index